Rej

Daily

Michelle Francl-Donnay
Jerome Kodell, OSB
Rachelle Linner
Ronald Witherup, PSS
Catherine Upchurch
Jay Cormier
Genevieve Glen, OSB

With an Introduction by Abbot John Klassen, OSB

LITURGICAL PRESS
Collegeville, Minnesota

www.litpress.org

Nihil Obstat: Reverend Robert Harren, J.C.L., *Censor deputatus.*
Imprimatur: ✠ Most Reverend Donald J. Kettler, J.C.L., Bishop of Saint Cloud, November 30, 2018.

Cover design by Monica Bokinskie. Cover art courtesy of Getty Images.

ISSN: 2578-7004 (Print)
ISSN: 2578-7012 (Online)

ISBN: 978-0-8146-4413-3   978-0-8146-4438-6 (e-book)

Introduction

Living through the Fifty Days of Easter

As Christians we find it spiritually intuitive to afford Ash Wednesday and the Lenten season, through the Triduum, to Easter Sunday a full measure of attention. We observe this season with intention, reflection, and a desire for conversion. The words of Ash Wednesday ring in our hearts: "Repent, and believe the Gospel!"

Over the years, in listening to the Scriptures and engaging with the liturgical season of the Fifty Days of Easter, I have come to understand the profound conversion that the disciples of Jesus and early Christians underwent in order to appropriate the full meaning of the dying and rising of Jesus. Repeatedly, we encounter the necessity of letting go of partial or mistaken understandings of Jesus' Messiahship; of embracing the power and freedom of the Holy Spirit and speaking a new language; of opening arms and hearts to be inclusive in understanding the liberating energy of being baptized into the dying and rising of Jesus.

I am thrilled by this publication because it offers readers and all who pray an opportunity to engage with a fresh, integrated, and provocative unpacking of the meaning of the Fifty Days for us, today.

Abbot John Klassen, OSB
Easter 2019

Reflections

Sentinels of the Dawn

Readings: Acts 10:34a, 37-43; Col 3:1-4 or 1 Cor 5:6b-8; John 20:1-9

Scripture:
When Christ your life appears,
   then you too will appear with him in glory. (Col 3:2)

Reflection: I'm standing on the porch at my brother's house. He lives high above a valley. Below me the dry bed of the Estrella River winds through cattle-dotted pastures and vineyards, a pale still life in the predawn light. Last night's stars have fled and the sky is streaked with color along the horizon. As I watch, a deep rosy glow grows in the east. I murmur a line from the *Benedictus*, "The dawn from on high shall break upon us, to shine on those who dwell in darkness . . ."

The sun bursts over the horizon, first a glint of gold, followed by such a fierce blaze that I cannot bear to look at it. I close my eyes and let the warmth wash over me. Such power, I marvel, that it can warm me from 93 million miles away, banishing the night's cold as with the flick of a finger.

Look to what is above, Paul advises the Colossians. This morning of all mornings, I'm tempted to read that literally. Look to what it is above, try to grasp the power and the glory that pour down on us at all times, day or night. We are called to be sentinels of the dawn, Pope Francis reminded us in a reflection on the Triduum. We are called to be the ones like Peter and Mary Magdalene who run to see signs of the Risen Christ. And if we can bear it, we are called to reflect that power and glory back for the world to see.

Meditation: Close your eyes and lift your face to the sun, feeling its warmth on your face. Where is Christ dawning in your life now? How might you reflect that glory for others to see?

Prayer: Christ, our light and our life, may your dawn warm our hearts, banish the darkness, and guide our feet into the way of peace, that we might at last wake to the fullness of your glory.

—Michelle Francl-Donnay

I Believe in the Holy Spirit

Readings: Acts 2:14, 22-33; Matt 28:8-15

Scripture:
Exalted at the right hand of God,
   he poured forth the promise of the Holy Spirit.
      (Acts 2:33a)

Reflection: *"I believe in the Holy Spirit . . ."* The words rise to my tongue each week, called forth between Word spoken and Body broken, borne aloft on the voices of friends and strangers. *"The Lord, the giver of life . . ."* I believe in the Spirit who once stirred in the chaos of creation, is stirring within me, within the world now. *"Who proceeds from the Father and the Son . . ."* One God, whose glory and majesty cannot be contained but spills over, pouring down from heaven onto earth.

It feels too soon to contemplate the coming of the Holy Spirit; the scent of incense from the Easter Vigil lingers in the corners of the church. The Easter season has barely dawned; Pentecost's flames are weeks away. I want to cling to these quiet moments, to the sure knowledge of the resurrection. But the reality is that my life is not some carefully choreographed and perfectly timed sequence of events. The fruits of the Spirit may be love, joy, peace, and patience, but the surest signs of the Spirit's passage are chaos and disruption. It is not too soon to be about the work of the Gospel.

We are all witnesses, says Peter. Go, tell the world. Go, says Jesus, bear my news to the disciples, tell them to get out of the room and on the road. Do not be afraid, says Jesus, for Father, Son, and Spirit will never leave you.

Meditation: We can be reluctant to embrace chaos, to let our lives be disrupted, even when the reasons are joyful. Where is the Spirit pushing you out of your comfort zone to be witness to the salvation of the world? What roads is Jesus suggesting you might walk with the Trinity this Easter season?

Prayer: Holy Spirit, who hovered over the waters at creation, breathe in us, that we might shout aloud our joy in the new life we have been given. Strengthen our hearts, that we might walk with firm purpose in God's ways.

—Michelle Francl-Donnay

April 23: Tuesday within the Octave of Easter

Pushing Through

Readings: Acts 2:36-41; John 20:11-18

Scripture:
But go to my brothers and tell them,
  "I am going to my Father and your Father,
  to my God and your God." (John 20:17b)

Reflection: St. Augustine called Mary Magdalene "the apostle to the apostles" because she was sent from the garden to tell the apostles the good news. Magdala means tower in Aramaic and I find the image of Mary the Tower a potent complement to Peter the Rock. The church may be built on the rock of Peter, but Mary of Magdala ignited it with these words: "I have seen the Lord."

Every time I hear this gospel I wonder what happened to Mary Magdalene next. Medieval legends say she retreated to pray in a cave in France, where she was fed by angels. The Orthodox Christian tradition places her with Mary, the Mother of God, in Ephesus.

"Go," Jesus told Mary Magdalene in the garden. I doubt Jesus meant for her to take a walk and deliver his message to the disciples and then vanish. *Poreuou*, the Greek word translated in today's gospel as "go," carries the sense of heading out on a journey. Its ultimate root is "pierced through." It is a call to reorder your life's direction, to push a message out into the world despite barriers and with a piercing clarity. *Go out*, Jesus demands of Mary Magdalene, *I want you to proclaim again and again, "I have seen the risen Lord."*

So I doubt Mary Magdalene stopped proclaiming the Good News when the disciples laughed at what they thought was nonsense, to quietly retire to a cave or a small house in Ephesus. I imagine her so aflame with the Gospel that wherever she went and whoever she met she could not help but deliver the message for all ages to come, "I have seen the risen Lord." And I cannot imagine that Christ expects me to do anything less.

Meditation: Who in your life is so afire with God's love that it spills over? What do you hear in Jesus' command to "go"? Are you willing to be aflame for the sake of the Gospel?

Prayer: Spirit of the living God, grant us clarity of vision, that we might see Christ in unexpected places. Grant us the courage to continually proclaim what we have seen: Christ is risen!

—Michelle Francl-Donnay

Love Seeks the Heights

Readings: Acts 3:1-10; Luke 24:13-35

Scripture:
Were not our hearts burning within us while he spoke
   to us on the way and opened the Scriptures to us?
   (Luke 24:32b)

Reflection: Our Orthodox brothers and sisters call it "Bright Week"—the eight days of Easter celebrated as if they were a single long day, spent together singing the liturgy with joy. The Liturgy of the Hours in the Roman Rite echoes this practice, repeating the psalms and antiphons of Easter throughout the octave.

The sacred and the secular rhythms of my life are so discordant in this week, where I go in a matter of five minutes from replaying Easter at Morning Prayer to office hours with stressed and exhausted students still facing the ordeal of final exams. Like the pair on the road to Emmaus, I'm not always sure what to make of these tensions, so I appreciate these moments of reflection and repetition scattered through my everyday life, with its potent mix of woundedness and wholeness, of trials and joy.

Christ breaks open the Scriptures for the disciples on the road to Emmaus, repeating the words of the prophets they would have known so well. He set their hearts on fire.

St. Augustine, in preaching on this gospel, encourages us also to be on fire—get yourselves white hot, says one translation—not just with faith, but with our works. *Let the flames whirl you up,* he says, *the passion of love will always seek the heights.*

The bones of Christ's call to me are clear, repeated again and again this week: *Hear me in the words of the prophets and psalmists. Know me in the breaking of the bread. Greet strangers as if they are me. Above all love, for love will whirl you up to the heights.*

Meditation: What Scripture passages set you aflame? What would such love move you to say to Jesus if you met him on the road?

Prayer: Jesus, in your death and resurrection you burned away our sins. Set us aflame, that we might find you in the Scriptures and in the Eucharist and serve you in those we meet along the road.

—Michelle Francl-Donnay

Paradoxical Easter

Readings: Acts 3:11-26; Luke 24:35-48

Scripture:
He stood in their midst and said to them,
"Peace be with you." (Luke 24:36b)

Reflection: Though eagerly gathered to hear the miraculous news that was being reported, the disciples were nevertheless terrified when that Good News appeared in front of them in all-too-real flesh. What seemed conceivable at one remove—perhaps it had been a ghost on the road to Emmaus—was suddenly, shatteringly, staggeringly present.

I can sympathize with the disciples, having once spent an Easter morning surrounded by families celebrating in their Easter finery and Easter afternoon at a funeral home greeting black-clad mourners at my husband's wake. I struggled to hear Christ's "Peace be with you" over the clamor of grief. I struggled that Easter to reconcile joy and sorrow, certainty and uncertainty. I struggle still.

In his book *Into the Silent Land*, Martin Laird, OSA, points out that, when we go in search of peace in prayer, we often find what feels like chaos. But, he says, it is precisely in this meeting of confusion and peace that healing happens—not by erasing our pain, but by opening a path for grace. The resurrection did not erase the pain of Christ's passion, nor does it take away our own travails. Even as I grappled with the paradox of that long ago Easter morning, the battle itself exposed the wounds to my soul.

I find in this gospel a space where those of us who are flustered by joy in sorrow, who are simultaneously mourning and rejoicing, can be healed. *Reach for me*, says Jesus. *Touch my wounds and do not be troubled any longer. For I am here with you, to the end of time.*

Meditation: In our everyday lives joy and sorrow, chaos and peace do not always follow the liturgical year. When have you felt out of kilter with the Easter season? How do you think Jesus might reach out to you in such moments?

Prayer: Grant us your peace, O Lord, in the midst of chaos and confusion. May we find our pain and sorrow leavened by joy and the sure knowledge of your presence with us all the days of our life.

—Michelle Francl-Donnay

April 26: Friday within the Octave of Easter

Handed On

Readings: Acts 4:1-12; John 21:1-14

Scripture:
Jesus said to them, "Come, have breakfast." (John 21:12a)

Reflection: As the weather turned cold and damp, I told my students that if they saw me at the local grocery store, they were welcome to ask for a lift back to campus. One of my students blurted out, "You grocery shop?" Somehow she couldn't imagine the same person who could use quantum mechanics to explain how particles go through walls also grocery shopped, made dinner, and did the laundry.

So when I read this gospel, and think, "Jesus made breakfast for them?" I too grasp the contradictions inherent in God-made-flesh, who could multiply loaves and fishes and call down manna from heaven to feed multitudes, crouching over an early morning fire, preparing fish and bread with his own hands.

Standing in my own kitchen, up to my elbows in soapy water cleaning up the remains of yet another meal, I realize that tucked away at the end of John's mystical gospel is a reminder of its beginning: that everything came into being through Jesus' hands, the ordinary as much as the extraordinary. The same hands that fashioned the universe, that opened the eyes of the blind, toasted bread.

In these Easter days of exultant glory, it is good to be reminded that the everyday is made sacred in Christ too. That just as Jesus fed the disciples with the miracle of his Body and Blood, he tended to their humble everyday needs as well: "Come, have breakfast." We are invited to see in the humble, everyday chores we all must do a chance to be the hands of God.

Meditation: What are you hungry for in your spiritual life? What might Jesus prepare for you that would satisfy that hunger? Which of the unappealing chores of daily life might be reborn for you in the light of this gospel?

Prayer: Jesus, the living bread who came down from heaven, we long to be fed at the many tables you prepare for us. Bless our hands, that they might joyfully undertake whatever work you need us to do today.

—Michelle Francl-Donnay

A Joy Complete

Readings: Acts 4:13-21; Mark 16:9-15

Scripture:
It is impossible for us not to speak about what we have seen
and heard. (Acts 4:20)

Reflection: Many years ago, a colleague of mine taught me
the traditional Orthodox paschal greeting, "Christ is risen!"
and its proper response, "He is risen indeed!" Each Easter-
tide when we ran into each other on campus, we would greet
each other in these words. As an unbelieving—or at least
unseeing—world bustled by, we joyfully affirmed what Mary
Magdalene knew that first Easter morning: Christ is risen.

At the Last Supper, Jesus reminded his disciple that joy is
his gift to us, "I have told you this so that my joy may be in
you and your joy may be complete" (John 15:11). In the fourth
movement of his Spiritual Exercises, St. Ignatius of Loyola
encourages us to immerse ourselves in Christ's experience
of the resurrection. This was an experience of such joy even
he could not contain it, entrusting it to Mary Magdalene in
the garden and the pair of travelers on the road in today's
gospel. They in turn could not contain their joy but poured
out the Good News to the apostles: "The Lord is alive!"

Easter's joy is not meant to be contemplated in silence,
held close within; nor is Easter's joy an end in and of itself.

This is a joy that demands to be acted on, fueling our words and our deeds, just as it drove Peter and John to the temple precincts to heal and to proclaim the incredible news of salvation.

Meditation: St. Francis of Assisi encourages us to preach the Gospel at all times, using words when we must. Where do you see the need to preach Easter's joy in word or in action? Where can you bring Jesus' healing grace to the world?

Prayer: Christ Jesus, may we always rejoice in your resurrection. Grant us the courage to proclaim the Gospel in word and deed and the grace to heal what is broken.

—Michelle Francl-Donnay

Faithful Doubts

Readings: Acts 5:12-16; Rev 1:9-11a, 12-13, 17-19; John 20:19-31

Scripture:
Put your finger here and see my hands,
    and bring your hand and put it into my side,
    and do not be unbelieving, but believe. (John 20:27)

Reflection: As a scientist, I don't fear doubt. It's part of my daily life, a routine reflective skepticism. A reminder that I might be wrong, doubt keeps me humble. More critically, doubt in science is a call to seek deeper truths, to push under the surface, to recognize that there is always more to learn. Doubt in science can also be a rich source of inspiration: Why does this molecule have such an odd structure? Is the experiment wrong or is there some new theory to be uncovered? Doubt pushes my work into new paths.

In my life of faith, I have come to see doubt equally as a gift. Doubt is, as theologian Paul Tillich would have it, not the opposite of faith but a critical part of a life of faith. Doubt keeps my faith humble; it's a recognition that faith is not of my own making but a gift. Doubt prompts me to scour my days for evidence of God at work, a routine of reflection that inevitably leads to another gift, gratitude. Doubt, the uncertainty inherent in our finite human inability to fully embrace the infinite Divine, reminds me there is always more of God to discover. Doubt changes me, pushing me onto new paths as it deepens my faith.

I am consoled by Jesus' response to Thomas in the gospel. Jesus doesn't mock Thomas for his doubts but tenderly invites him to come closer. *Don't look the other way, face your doubts, face me*, Jesus says to Thomas and to us. Doubt draws me again and again into an encounter with the living God. What greater gift could there be?

Meditation: What doubts do you fear most? Confide them to Jesus and imagine his response to you. What gift is he offering in the midst of these doubts?

Prayer: God of wisdom and compassion, we long for certainty in the midst of doubt. Open our eyes to see your work in our lives, that we might be ever grateful for your gifts. Draw us more deeply into your life.

—Michelle Francl-Donnay

Pentecost People

Readings: Acts 4:23-31; John 3:1-8

Scripture:
As they prayed, the place where they were gathered shook,
    and they were all filled with the Holy Spirit
    and continued to speak the word of God with boldness.
    (Acts 4:31)

Reflection: The chief priests and elders had a problem on their hands. Peter and John were making a stir. People were getting excited. The officials thought a little show of authority would silence these two fishermen, "uneducated, ordinary men" (Acts 4:13). But the apostles were not subdued at all by the action of the authorities. They went back to their own people even more enthusiastic and optimistic. They prayed, asking the Lord for boldness in continuing to proclaim Jesus. The place shook, and they were all filled with the Holy Spirit. The disciples experienced this coming of the Spirit as a new boost for their Christian journey. This sounds very much like what happened at Pentecost, and in fact it is, because the outpouring of the Holy Spirit didn't just happen one time and stop.

The reading from the Gospel of John tells how it happens in another way, a more subtle and elusive way, when "you do not know where it comes from or where it goes." This is the more common experience, the almost imperceptible sound of the "still, small voice," rather than a visitation that rattles the walls. The point is that the Spirit is not finished with this work, and that work is us.

Meditation: Today might be a good time to look back at times in your own life when you have felt a renewal of hope or enthusiasm, maybe in prayer, or in an experience of beauty, or in communion with a person. That breeze was the Holy Spirit.

Prayer: Come to me, Holy Spirit, and help me to be responsive, whether you shake my walls or only ruffle my hair. First of all, make me attentive to your action in the daily comings and goings in my life and aware of your presence in the people I meet. Make me porous and transparent so that you may pass through me to others who need your love as much as I do.

—Jerome Kodell, OSB

April 30: Tuesday of the Second Week of Easter

Children of Encouragement

Readings: Acts 4:32-37; John 3:7b-15

Scripture:
The community of believers was of one heart and mind,
   and no one claimed that any of his possessions was
      his own,
   but they had everything in common. (Acts 4:32)

Reflection: The Christian community gathered in Jerusalem is presented in all its beauty, united in peace and love. In today's first reading we are introduced to a disciple who embodied this ideal and even in his nickname, Barnabas, "son of encouragement," reflected the true Christian spirit. Our reverie will be quickly adjusted, however, by the story of the couple Ananias and Sapphira, which immediately follows this example of communal unity. They betray the trust of the community, holding back property while pretending to be giving all they have.

In his poem "Nothing Gold Can Stay," Robert Frost describes the yellow shade of a tiny spring leaf before it turns green. He proceeds to apply this to the excitement and sheen of all new beginnings, which levels out to the humdrum as the season progresses. Acts of the Apostles does not hide the fact that the first fervor did not last very long. Soon after the

Ananias and Sapphira episode, we read of the inequity experienced by the Hellenist widows (Acts 6:1).

But in both of these cases, the whitecaps of dissension did not sink the ship. The community dealt with the trouble and then continued the journey, confident of the Lord's presence and guidance.

Meditation: Hardly a day goes by when there is not a disappointment to challenge our dreams. The constant stream of news from all corners of the world often focuses on bad news, which attracts attention better than good news. This leaves in its wake shattered dreams about our country, the church, the world. Add to this the disappointment in ourselves because of personal failures. How can you follow the example of the early Christians, to repair what you can and continue to persevere, knowing that it is God who is "able to accomplish far more than all we ask or imagine" (Eph 3:20)?

Prayer: Heavenly Father, we call out to you in the prayer of our father in faith, Sirach: "Come to our aid, O God of the universe. . . . Hear the prayer of your servants, according to your good will toward your people. Thus all the ends of the earth will know that you are the eternal God" (Sir 36:1, 22).

—Jerome Kodell, OSB

The Light of Truth

Readings: Acts 5:17-26; John 3:16-21

Scripture:
Whoever lives the truth comes to the light,
  so that his works may be clearly seen as done in God.
    (John 3:21)

Reflection: Some years ago a French politician was caught in a lie about his actions. His defense was: "I lied in good faith." The distortion is so blatant it takes our breath away. Sadly, the abuse of truth in public life has only increased with time, and we are not surprised any more by dishonesty in national and international leaders. Perjury is still on the books as a felony, but it is seldom prosecuted. We are plagued by "fake truth," which may at most receive a slap on the wrist.

Jesus minces no words about truth. "The truth will set you free" (John 8:32), but denying or avoiding it is to live in darkness. Truth is not just a concept, a correlation of facts and statements. Jesus identifies himself as the truth incarnate and says that his followers will be guided by the "Spirit of truth" (John 16:13). The devil, on the other hand, is the "father of lies" (John 8:44).

Cardinal John Henry Newman understood the Christian vocation as commitment to the truth and said that living the faith conscientiously is like carrying a holy flame: "In a dark world Truth still makes its way in spite of the darkness, passing from hand to hand."

Meditation: The assault on truth in our culture makes it harder to live a life of integrity. In times past, people were able to say, "My word is my bond." They meant it, and everyone knew they meant it, because it contained a sense of personal honor. The fact that truth is fading as a value in our culture does not mean that its validity has changed. The truth is still the truth, and the truth will still set us free. As one of Jesus' disciples, how can you live the truth as a gift to the world?

Prayer: O God, send forth again your Spirit of truth into our world. Help our culture to appreciate again the beauty of integrity and to value those who speak and live the truth. Awake in me a new dedication to a life of faithfulness in word and deed, and let your truth shine through me to all I meet.

—Jerome Kodell, OSB

May 2: Saint Athanasius,
Bishop and Doctor of the Church

The Family of God

Readings: Acts 5:27-33; John 3:31-36

Scripture:
We are witnesses of these things,
  as is the Holy Spirit whom God has given to those who
    obey him. (Acts 5:32)

Reflection: The early Christians had a strong sense of intimacy with God and with one another as the family or household of God. Here they see themselves as fellow witnesses with the Holy Spirit. Later in Acts, when transmitting the decision of the Jerusalem Council concerning admission of the Gentiles, the leaders write, "It is the decision of the holy Spirit and of us" (15:28), which would be arrogant if it were not so natural. When new members joined them, they were said to be added not "in the community" but "in the Lord" (Acts 5:14).

This sense of intimacy in the family of God is not limited to the Acts of the Apostles but pervades the New Testament: "you are fellow citizens with the holy ones and members of the household of God" (Eph 2:19), and even "share in the divine nature" (2 Pet 1:4). In Paul's theology of the Body of Christ, there is a development from disciples being individually parts of the body (1 Cor 12:27) to being "individually parts of one another" (Rom 12:5).

Anyone who views Christianity as a philosophy or a set of rules has only to read the New Testament to understand that it is a life, a life centered in Christ and through him a participation in the trinitarian life.

Meditation: People who join the Catholic Church from other denominations rarely do so as a conversion to Jesus Christ, with whom they are already united by faith, but often rather to the tradition that has preserved the family relationship experienced in the early church. How do you experience a sense of family within the church?

Prayer: Dear God, we rejoice in the new covenant in the blood of Christ, which breaks all boundaries and unites us in the Body of Christ with Christians all over the world and even into eternity. We ask for a new appreciation of the intimacy God has given us with himself, permitting us to align ourselves naturally with the Holy Spirit in praying to the Father in Christ.

—Jerome Kodell, OSB

Standing in the Gospel

Readings: 1 Cor 15:1-8; John 14:6-14

Scripture:
I am reminding you, brothers and sisters,
   of the Gospel I preached to you,
      which you indeed received and in which you also stand.
      (1 Cor 15:1)

Reflection: St. Paul used the term "Gospel" long before the gospels of Matthew, Mark, Luke, and John were written. Here the term has its original meaning of the "good news" about Jesus Christ and is synonymous with "the word I preached to you" in the following verse. Paul summarizes that good news in a very quick overview of the basics of the faith.

When Paul says we are "standing" in the Gospel he is not referring to a book or even a summary of the good news, but to the Christ-event, which is the good news beyond anything written down. In his postsynodal document The Word of God in the Church (*Verbum Domini*, 2010), Pope Benedict XVI wrote that Christianity is not a "religion of the book" but the "religion of the word of God." To "stand in the Gospel" is not only to be well instructed in the teaching of the Bible, but to read it and everything else in Christian history "in the stream of the apostolic Tradition from which it is inseparable" (par. 7).

The Word of God produced the church, and the church produced the Bible as the authentic mirror of her living faith. Thus we read the Bible "in the Church" (Constitution on the Sacred Liturgy, par. 7), that is, in the stream of the Tradition, in order to stand in the Gospel.

Meditation: There are many voices clamoring for our attention in this world. How do you discern the authentic word in the cacophony of competing positions? Perhaps in pre-internet days people were not subjected to the barrage of opinions that has become our daily fare, but it has always been a challenge to know who and what to believe. Christ intends the church to be "the pillar and foundation of truth" (1 Tim 3:15), not by intellectual prowess but by relying on the promised guidance of the Holy Spirit.

Prayer: Heavenly Father, we praise you for having sent your Word into the world and revealed through him the truth for life and salvation. Inspire our leaders and teachers as they bring this Word to us, and open our hearts to receive it and stand in the Gospel.

—Jerome Kodell, OSB

The Barque of Peter

Readings: Acts 6:1-7; John 6:16-21

Scripture:
When they had rowed about three or four miles,
   they saw Jesus walking on the sea and coming near
      the boat,
   and they began to be afraid.
But he said to them, "It is I. Do not be afraid." (John 6:19-20)

Reflection: One of the oldest symbols for the church is the barque or boat of Peter, a wind-tossed vessel with Peter at the helm and Jesus a passenger. Jesus was quite clear that his followers could expect to suffer for being at odds with the values of the "ruler of this world" (John 14:30), and we know that the church has experienced a stormy history. At times some of Jesus' followers have given up on the church because of its human leadership or the sins of its members. Others have despaired completely of its survival. The symbol of the church as a boat with Jesus aboard gives hope and encouragement.

   Jesus is not aboard as the scene is described in John, but he is walking beside the boat on the water. In the versions of Matthew and Mark, Jesus gets into the boat, and there are other variations as well. But what is common to all three accounts are Jesus' reassuring words, "It is I. Do not be afraid." These two statements have a long history in the biblical tradition and would have been immediately recognized by the apostles. They proclaim a divine visitation and presence, not a threatening presence, but a loving presence that casts out fear. The presence of Jesus makes the boat a safe place, no matter what storms might be brewing.

Throughout church history the image of the barque of Peter has brought encouragement in times of crisis, and it serves us again today in the eruption of the sexual abuse crisis. The church has recovered time and time again and will do so again, though we don't know how. But we fear not, because Christ is with us.

Meditation: How can the image of the barque of Peter bring reassurance to you in the midst of crisis?

Prayer: Jesus, we are on a stormy sea, but we are able to go forward hopefully because we are confident you are with us on this journey. But we are frail and need constant encouragement, and we call on you to speak to our hearts and strengthen our faith as we go on together.

—Jerome Kodell, OSB

May 5: Third Sunday of Easter

The Lamb That Was Slain

Readings: Acts 5:27-32; 40b-41; Rev 5:11-14; John 21:1-19

Scripture:
Worthy is the Lamb that was slain
 to receive power and riches, wisdom and strength,
 honor and glory and blessing. (Rev 5:12)

Reflection: The heavenly scene centers on the Lamb standing on the throne of God, surrounded by the four living creatures, representing all animate creation, and the twenty-four elders, the patriarchs and the apostles representing all the people of God. But the figure of this Lamb jars with the popular image of a lamb as a gentle, cuddly animal. This is a "Lamb that was slain" and still has the marks of his ordeal.

We recognize this Lamb as the risen Jesus, who has won our salvation in his victory over death. But why does Jesus still bear the marks of suffering? We note the same in the account of his appearance to the disciples after the resurrection, when Thomas must put his finger and hand into the wounds of Jesus. These are now glorified wounds, but they are still visible, because the resurrection does not erase the memory of Jesus' human experience. It is because he still remembers his experience among us that we can approach him confidently: "Because he himself was tested through what he suffered, he is able to help those who are being tested" (Heb 2:18).

A popular version of the Christian message these days is what is known as the Prosperity Gospel. In basic terms, this teaches that a life of faith in Jesus Christ will be rewarded by health and wealth. This is so far from the teaching of Jesus and his own image in the gospels that it might seem to be a spoof. But a Pew Forum poll some years ago found that 46 percent of self-identified US Christians agreed with the statement: God will grant material prosperity to all believers who have enough faith.

The image of the slain Lamb brings us back to reality, reminding us of Jesus' words, "Whoever wishes to come after me must deny himself, take up his cross, and follow me" (Mark 8:34).

Meditation: The image of the slain Lamb gives us realistic expectations of being Christians. How can you strive to meet these expectations in your daily life?

Prayer: O God our Father, in giving his life for our salvation, your Son modeled for us how we must live if we wish to join him in heaven. Guide and help each of us take up our cross and follow the slain Lamb to the kingdom.

—Jerome Kodell, OSB

Filled with Grace and Power

Readings: Acts 6:8-15; John 6:22-29

Scripture:
Stephen, filled with grace and power,
  was working great wonders and signs among the people.
Certain members . . .
  came forward and debated with Stephen,
  but they could not withstand the wisdom and the Spirit
    with which he spoke. (Acts 6:8-10)

Reflection: Trusted by the community of the disciples, the first named of the seven deacons, Stephen, is described as "a man full of faith and the holy Spirit" (Acts 6:5). Stephen was a Hellenist, a Greek-speaking Jew who became a Christian convert. He was a man abundantly blessed with faith and good works, gifts from the Holy Spirit, given to people, not for their own use, but to build up the community.

Stephen assumed a leadership role when his community faced a particularly difficult time. Something new had arisen, something that challenged old definitions of orthodoxy. Something at once attractive and threatening. Something about theology and creed that created rifts in families and among friends.

Change is always difficult, and sometimes we forget that what exists now was also once new.

Many years ago in a parish discussion group I met a World War II veteran who had gone to Mass on nine First Fridays because he was promised that he would be able to make an act of contrition before he died. This assurance was a great comfort to him during the war. Years later, still a faithful churchgoer, he was uncomfortable with many of the changes after Vatican II. He didn't recognize what the church had become. In his frustration he angrily confronted a startled parish priest and demanded to know, "Will I still be able to make an act of contrition before I die?"

I have never forgotten the pain in his voice as he grieved the loss of a particular kind of holiness. Maybe some of Stephen's community felt the same way.

Meditation: With baptism, we receive the incalculable gift of the Holy Spirit, becoming members of the Body of Christ. It can take time for our gifts to develop, and sometimes we need others to show us the gifts we do not see. Today, think about your gifts and how you use them to build up the community that is the church.

Prayer: Lord, we give thanks for people like Stephen who speak courageously in spite of opposition. Help us to recognize and support the Stephens who serve in our midst today.

—Rachelle Linner

Martyrdom

Readings: Acts 7:51–8:1a; John 6:30-35

Scripture:
Lord, do not hold this sin against them. (Acts 7:60)

Reflection: St. Stephen was the church's first martyr. Today we are facing what journalist John Allen calls a "global pandemic of anti-Christian violence and persecution." Pope Francis has commented that this new wave of martyrdom is an "ecumenism of blood," indiscriminately affecting Catholic, Protestant, and Orthodox Christians.

The litany of suffering inflicted on these new martyrs includes mob-inspired violence, rape, kidnapping, dubious claims of blasphemy, terrorist bombings, and social and economic restrictions. While mainly occurring in Asia and Africa, it can also happen in Catholic countries. Witness the life and death of St. Oscar Romero, who died, according to Pope Francis, because of "hatred for a faith that, imbued with charity, would not be silent in the face of the injustices that relentlessly and cruelly slaughtered the poor and their defenders." Or the lesser-known Pino Puglisi, a Sicilian priest who was killed by the Mafia in 1993 and beatified as a martyr twenty years later.

Depending on the source of the statistic, estimates of Christian suffering vary greatly, from seven thousand to one hundred thousand annual deaths. It can be easy to become numbed by those numbers, which is why it is important to hear individual stories.

On Christmas Day 2011, forty-five people died in a bomb blast at St. Theresa's Church in Madalla, Nigeria. Among them were Chioma Dike's husband and three of her five children. In a 2015 interview, Mrs. Dike says she has no hatred for the Boko Haram terrorists who carried out the bombing. She is quoted as saying, "I'm not angry. . . . I pray for God to forgive them, because they don't know what they are doing."

St. Stephen's martyrdom imitated Jesus' trial and death: eloquent speech, charges of blasphemy, and, most important, forgiveness of his persecutors. It is remarkable to hear our contemporaries repeat that decisive plea, the distinguishing characteristic of Christianity.

Meditation: The great twentieth-century Protestant theologian Karl Barth famously said that one should do theology "with the Bible in one hand, and the newspaper in the other." Do you find stories in this week's newspaper that resonate with the story of St. Stephen's martyrdom? How are they similar? How are they different?

Prayer: Lord, give us the grace to forgive those who trespass against us.

—Rachelle Linner

From Persecution to Proclamation

Readings: Acts 8:1b-8; John 6:35-40

Scripture:
With one accord, the crowds paid attention to what was
  said by Philip
  when they heard it and saw the signs he was doing.
For unclean spirits, crying out in a loud voice,
  came out of many possessed people,
  and many paralyzed and crippled people were cured.
There was great joy in that city. (Acts 8:6-8)

Reflection: The persecution of the Jerusalem church led to
the scattering of the disciples and the preaching of the Word.
Something terrible led to something that brought "great joy"
to many in Samaria. If there had been no persecution, the
church would have grown and developed in a much different way. The forced exile led to a powerful evangelization.

Since that time the history of the church has vividly il-
lustrated Jesus' teaching that "unless a grain of wheat falls
to the ground and dies, it remains just a grain of wheat; but
if it dies, it produces much fruit" (John 12:24). Or, as Tertul-
lian wrote, "The blood of martyrs is the seed of the Church."

It is like that in our own lives too. We can suddenly find
ourselves facing a terrible calamity, whether from fire or
flood, serious illness, loss of work, financial hardships, or

difficult relationships. Our sense of safety and security, our confidence in ourselves and our gifts, is overwhelmed by an awareness of the stark poverty and sheer vulnerability of being human.

No one asks for these things, but when they happen the grain of wheat that surrounds our pride and self-sufficiency falls to the ground and dies. And slowly, without knowing how, something fruitful can emerge from our suffering. We may discover that we had worshiped idols of security or success that led us far from our vocation. We may find a new empathy for others, perhaps those who are vulnerable because of race or religion. In the truth of the beatitude, we who mourned now rejoice, and we are clothed in a hard-won humility and a genuine enduring faith.

We are scattered, in exile from our true homeland, but with grace our ears might be open to hear and our eyes to see the signs of God's magnificent power and grace. And, like the people of Samaria, we will know great joy.

Meditation: Have you ever experienced something positive emerging from a difficult time? Do your own daily dyings and risings deepen your response to the paschal mystery we celebrate this Easter season?

Prayer: Lord, we can be paralyzed and crippled by so many things. Grant us ears to hear your liberating word.

—Rachelle Linner

Get Up

Readings: Acts 8:26-40; John 6:44-51

Scripture:
The angel of the Lord spoke to Philip,
  "Get up and head south on the road
  that goes down from Jerusalem to Gaza, the desert route."
So he got up and set out. (Acts 8:26-27)

Reflection: Because Philip obeys so wholeheartedly, faithfully, and promptly, an Ethiopian eunuch is led to understanding a puzzling passage of Scripture, is immersed in the waters of baptism, and goes on his way rejoicing. This remarkable story from Acts offers a compelling image of the growth of the church, from its early days until today. There have always been people like Philip who are willing to give up everything in obedience to God's call, even when the call offers few details. Surely he couldn't have known who or what he would find on that desert route.

God still calls people to be Philips to each other. It can happen at any time, wherever we happen to be, whatever role we play in society or in the church. All at once we are surprised to find ourselves speaking a word, maybe to a person who is a stranger to us. When we have those moments we can be sure that, like Philip, we are being sent.

Philip is brave, but so is the Ethiopian eunuch, because he searches for religious truth with diligence. There is a plaintive humility when he answers Philip that he cannot understand "unless someone instructs me." Even today, with such an abundance of information, we can only go so far on our own. We need someone else to assuage our deepest hungers, to hear the questions behind the questions. Someone to stop when we see water on a desert road and help to bring us to new life through the grace of renewed baptismal vows, the gift of a well-lived Lent and a joyous Easter season.

Meditation: Do you identify more with Philip or with the Ethiopian eunuch? Can you think of a time when you have been like Philip, surprised to find yourself someplace, not sure how you got there, but knowing you were responding to a call? Can you think of a time when you have been like the eunuch, needing and finding a teacher?

Prayer: Lord, give us the faith to go where you send us, the humility to know when we are in need of teachers, and the grace to open our eyes to the water that surrounds us, even on desert roads.

—Rachelle Linner

Regained Sight

Readings: Acts 9:1-20; John 6:52-59

Scripture:
So Ananias went and entered the house;
  laying his hands on him, he said,
  "Saul, my brother, the Lord has sent me,
  Jesus who appeared to you on the way by which
    you came,
  that you may regain your sight and be filled with the
    Holy Spirit."
Immediately things like scales fell from his eyes
  and he regained his sight. (Acts 9:17-18)

Reflection: The conversion of Saul is told three times in Acts. The story we hear today is the historical narrative, a straight-forward account describing his encounter with the risen Jesus, temporary blindness, meeting with Ananias, recovery of sight, and baptism. In Acts 22 Paul tells the story, in Hebrew, to his fellow Jews, and in chapter 26 he tells it again as part of his defense in front of the Roman authorities.

Not surprisingly, the phrase "on the road to Damascus" has become shorthand for a radical conversion. It is hard to imagine the extraordinary change this ushered in for Saul, how over the course of three days he went from being an opponent of Christianity to one of its most inspired advocates. The life-changing character of this event is probably why Acts tells it twice more and why Paul must have prayed over and thought about it countless times, as he lived out the action and suffering that came from that encounter.

Most people can name a similar experience when God has intervened in their lives, albeit probably not in the same dramatic way that it happened for Saul. We should allow ourselves to savor those encounters. We should return to them in prayer, remembering where we were when the Lord spoke to us. We should try to remember what his voice, or his silence, was like. We should remember how we were changed by his word, how people around us reacted when they realized we were different. Such remembering is a way of giving thanks, again and again, for God's longing for us.

Meditation: Have you ever had a road-to-Damascus experience? Was there an Ananias who was sent to lead you on a new path? Were you ever an Ananias for someone else? Remember and revisit these times in prayer, savoring God's care on your journey.

Prayer: Lord, every time we receive your Body and Blood in the Eucharist we meet you as truly as Saul met you in the flashing light. May the scales fall from our eyes and our sight be restored by this sacred encounter.

—Rachelle Linner

May 11: Saturday of the Third Week of Easter

Rise Up

Readings: Acts 9:31-42; John 6:60-69

Scripture:
Peter sent them all out and knelt down and prayed.
Then he turned to her body and said, "Tabitha, rise up."
She opened her eyes, saw Peter, and sat up.
He gave her his hand and raised her up,
    and when he had called the holy ones and the widows,
    he presented her alive.
This became known all over Joppa,
    and many came to believe in the Lord. (Acts 9:40-42)

Reflection: Tabitha, which translates as Dorcas, was a disciple, a woman "completely occupied with good deeds and almsgiving." We don't need to imagine the grief people felt when Dorcas died. We have the tender portrait in Acts, the widows standing beside Peter, weeping for their friend, showing him the garments she had made. I wonder if Peter, with his roughened fisherman's fingers, could have appreciated the fine cloth that Dorcas had woven. Even if he couldn't judge the quality of her craft, he surely understood her life as a disciple. Her path—fidelity to Jesus and to the church—was the same as his.

It is this worthy woman whom Peter raises, a miracle that is reminiscent of Elijah and the widow's son at Zarephath

(1 Kgs 17:17-24) and Elisha raising the son of the Shunam-mite woman (2 Kgs 4:32-26). In both of those stories the resurrection requires vigorous physical activity. Elijah stretches out on the child three times while he cried to the Lord. Similarly, Elisha lies on the boy's body, paces around the room, and stretches out on the boy again. The resurrection of Dorcas is simpler and quieter.

Did the two men of Joppa go to Peter with the intention of asking him to raise Dorcas? Was Peter moved by their faith or frightened of it? In Lydda Peter healed Aeneas, a man paralyzed eight years, not by his prayers but with the words "Jesus Christ heals you." The raising of Dorcas, through his own prayer, is a much different miracle. Did he imagine, when he went to the upper room, what would happen? Or was this act the intervention of God as a means of bringing others to believe in the Lord?

Meditation: How do you think about miracles? Do stories like this make you uncomfortable? Can you remember a situation when the good deeds and almsgiving of someone led to a miraculous resurgence of hope and newness of life for someone? Would you count that as a miracle?

Prayer: Lord, may our "good deeds and almsgiving" bring comfort to those who weep today.

—Rachelle Linner

Being Known

Readings: Acts 13:14, 43-52; Rev 7:9, 14b-17; John 10:27-30

Scripture:
Jesus said:
"My sheep hear my voice;
   I know them, and they follow me.
I give them eternal life, and they shall never perish."
   (John 10:27-28)

Reflection: Today's gospel is taken from the end of the long, theologically rich Good Shepherd discourse in the tenth chapter of John's gospel.

At first glance, it's a little discordant. Told that the sheep hear the shepherd's voice, one would expect the next phrase to be "they know me, and they follow me." Instead, we learn that it is the shepherd who knows his sheep, and they follow. It is unexpected and a little disappointing. Don't we spend time and effort trying to listen to the voice of the Good Shepherd, so we can know and follow him with greater love and integrity?

This text suggests that the sheep follow the shepherd because they are known. The psalmist gloriously affirms what it is to be known by God: "I praise you, because I am wonderfully made; / wonderful are your works! / My very self you know. / My bones are not hidden from you, / When I was being made in secret, / fashioned in the depths of the earth" (Ps 139:14-15).

It can be difficult to know if we are hearing God's Word, especially in times as noisy as these. A good guideline for judging the authenticity of what we hear is to ask: Does the voice we hear allow us to be known? Does it lessen our tenacious hold on pride, vainglory, or greed? Do we let go, at least a little, of the false self we present to the world, the carapace that protects our fragile egos, that lets us appear self-sufficient or remarkable?

If the Word we hear allows us to be vulnerable and known, then we can trust it is the Good Shepherd we are hearing. Knowing we are safe in his care, we can follow and rejoice.

Meditation: Praying with Scripture is, for many, the most privileged way we learn to recognize the voice of the Good Shepherd. But we can also hear his voice in liturgy, through church teaching, in our most intimate relationships, when contemplating nature, or rapt in music or art. Where and how do you hear his voice?

Prayer: Lord, teach us to hear your voice so we can follow you with trust and confidence.

—Rachelle Linner

Limits to God's Grace?

Readings: Acts 11:1-18; John 10:1-10

Scripture:
If then God gave them the same gift he gave to us
   when we came to believe in the Lord Jesus Christ,
   who was I to be able to hinder God? (Acts 11:17)

Reflection: Setting limits or boundaries helps people feel more secure. We see it in the resurgence of nationalism and protectionism on the international scene. We also see it in the return of an "us versus them" mentality that has crept into the contemporary American mind-set.

God's tendency, however, is to expand the limits. Take the story from Acts that we hear in today's first reading. Through God's grace, Peter receives the insight that the Holy Spirit was intended for the Gentiles as well as the Jews. Imagine what it must have been like for someone like Peter, a devout Jew who believed God had chosen Israel as God's special people, to realize that others were to be included in the kingdom too. Prior to this revelation, Peter was merely trying to follow the Jewish laws to avoid unclean foods tainted from possible Gentile pagan rituals. The heavenly voice changes that perception, telling him three times during his prayer, "What God has made clean, you are not to call profane." Who was he to countermand God's voice? So, he follows through with the visit to the Gentiles and leaves with the realization that the same Holy Spirit guiding his life has now been bestowed on the Gentiles. Outsiders have become insiders!

Meditation: Reflect on the people whom you consider outsiders today. What places them in this category? How do you think God views them?

Prayer: Good and gracious Father in heaven, you have willed to draw all to yourself by the gift of the Holy Spirit and by sharing your love with all humanity. Enlarge our vision, Lord, so that we might become more welcoming of all those you invite to your heavenly banquet.

—Ronald Witherup, PSS

To Be Chosen

Readings: Acts 1:15-17, 20-26; John 15:9-17

Scripture:
It was not you who chose me, but I who chose you
  and appointed you to go and bear fruit that will remain.
    (John 15:16)

Reflection: Sometimes people are surprised to see in the gospels that discipleship is not for volunteers. Rather, as Jesus' words indicate in today's gospel, he chooses us, not the other way around. Even the story of Matthias told in the first reading reveals this truth. In order to maintain the symbolic number of twelve apostles—tied to the hope of judging the twelve tribes of Israel—the disciples trust the Holy Spirit to choose a replacement for Judas Iscariot, who betrayed Jesus. The lot falls to Matthias, whose feast we celebrate today. His being chosen not only completes the circle of twelve once more but also opens up the path of discipleship for all succeeding generations of believers.

Why is discipleship not merely a matter of volunteering? Would that not indicate our willingness, our openness to serve God and God's people? Such an attitude would reduce discipleship to a mere job, a personal preference for which we could expect to be compensated. Discipleship is not like that. It rests on a vocation. Jesus chooses disciples, sometimes from among the most unlikely candidates. God often invites people from the margins of society or unexpected places for important ministry.

One of my favorite artistic portrayals of the call of a disciple is Caravaggio's famous *Call of Saint Matthew*. It can be seen in a small side chapel at the French-speaking church in Rome, San Luigi dei Francesi. Jesus points to Matthew sitting at his tax collector's table filled with money. Matthew looks at Jesus, his left hand pointing back to himself, as if to say, "Are you talking to *me*?"

That is indeed how vocation works. One is called and sent out on mission.

Meditation: To what is God calling you as a disciple in your life? Do you feel up to the task? Does it frighten you, surprise you, startle you? What "fruit" do you hope to bear by responding yes to the Lord's call?

Prayer: Lord Jesus, my Lord and Savior, I am honored to be chosen by you, and I place myself in your hands. If I am sometimes reluctant to go where you would send me, I trust that you will guide and accompany me along the true path. Stay with me Lord, especially in challenging times, and I will do my best to stay with you.

—Ronald Witherup, PSS

May 15: Wednesday of the Fourth Week of Easter

Light Still Shines in the Darkness

Readings: Acts 12:24–13:5a; John 12:44-50

Scripture:
I came into the world as light,
  so that everyone who believes in me might not remain
    in darkness. (John 12:46)

Reflection: Darkness can speak to both young and old. Little children are often afraid of the dark. Some even have difficulty falling asleep at night in a darkened room because they fear "monsters" lurking in the darkness. As for adults, we know well that those who are up to no good prefer to do it under cover of darkness. They don't want to be seen, and so they hide their unworthy deeds. Darkness provides cover.

Light and darkness are more than a physical reality, though. The contrasting images of light and darkness remain an enduring metaphor that most people appreciate. Have you ever experienced a dinner by candlelight? It creates a romantic and desirable atmosphere. Those who attended the Easter Vigil a few weeks ago—hopefully, well done on Holy Saturday evening after sunset—will recall the dramatic contrast of lighting the new fire and then following the Easter candle into a darkened church that slowly became illuminated by the lighting of candles, accompanied by the chant of "Christ our Light."

Jesus in the Gospel of John speaks frequently of light and darkness. He is the "light of the world," and he came so that we human beings, who so often prefer to remain in our darkness, would no longer need to do so. The entire Easter season celebrates this light that abides forever.

Meditation: What aspects of "darkness" still remain in your own life? Try experiencing light and darkness in a prayer exercise. In a darkened room, sit quietly for a time before a lighted candle and appreciate the contrasting shadows it produces. You might make a mantra prayer of "Christ our Light, enlighten my life!" as you meditate on the beauty of the light penetrating the darkness.

Prayer: Christ our Light, do not let us remain in the darkness of our lives. You came so that we might be enlightened, and we place ourselves in your care. Light the path that leads to your kingdom, and help us lead others along the same path, so that all may benefit from the light you bring into the world, the light that endures forever and ever.

—Ronald Witherup, PSS

May 16: Thursday of the Fourth Week of Easter

Masters and Messengers

Readings: Acts 13:13-25; John 13:16-20

Scripture:
Amen, amen, I say to you, no slave is greater than his master
   nor any messenger greater than the one who sent him.
      (John 13:16)

Reflection: When I was a full-time teacher, one of the joys I had was to see former students return for visits and to recount all that they had achieved in their lives since graduation. It was particularly affirming to hear testimony that something I had said or demanded of them in class had made a difference. Mind you, this does not happen too often!

In today's gospel, which occurs after Jesus had washed his disciples' feet, Jesus reflects on the roles of masters and the messengers they send out. He had concretely shown them what it meant to be a servant (also translated as "slave") when he washed their feet. They were to do likewise. But it is not easy to imitate the master in this humble way. People generally seek to establish their own status, their own identity, their own accomplishments. Yet, the relationship between master and servant is intimate. Jesus points out: "whoever receives the one I send receives me, and whoever receives me receives the one who sent me" (John 13:20). What we do is in the name of the master, not our own name.

What we proclaim is his message, not our own. Our task is to lead others to know the master, the Lord Jesus, by our words and deeds. If and when we do this, then we will have fulfilled our task as true servants.

Meditation: Being a disciple is entering into a kind of missionary chain in which each person plays a role in the service of a larger entity. How do you perceive your own mission as a disciple of Jesus Christ? How can you communicate him better by your words, thoughts, and deeds? Think of ways to become a better disciple.

Prayer: Lord Jesus, you have shown me the way to serve and have called me to imitate your own selfless giving for others. I thank you most sincerely for sharing this divine mission. I ask your grace to give impetus to my words and actions so that they will be more effective and will lead others to know you for the loving Master you are. Blessed be your name now and forever!

—Ronald Witherup, PSS

The Way, the Truth, the Life

Readings: Acts 13:26-33; John 14:1-6

Scripture:
Thomas said to him,
  "Master, we do not know where you are going;
  how can we know the way?"
Jesus said to him, "I am the way and the truth and the life.
No one comes to the Father except through me."
  (John 14:5-6)

Reflection: An acquaintance once told me a tale of driving through rural Ireland on a vacation when he came to a fork in the road. In the distance, he could see a village that was where he wanted to go, but he was not sure which of the two roads led there. Luckily, he saw a young man casually leaning against a barn next to the road, chewing on a blade of grass and seemingly watching the world go by. So he asked him which road he should take to get to the village. The response was unexpected: "Oh, whichever one you take, you'll wish you'd taken the other!"

In the spiritual life, Jesus has given us more than just a road map to the kingdom. He has given all that is needed—himself! Get to know him, and you get to know his heavenly Father. The words in today's gospel are very familiar. But what does it really mean to call Jesus the Way, the Truth, and the Life? The way implies the proper path (the "how," we might say) to get to the Father and his kingdom. The Truth represents the content (the "what") embodied in the person of Jesus, whose very existence leads to the Father whence he came. And the Life represents the goal (the "why") of Jesus' coming into the world. He came so that we might have abundant and eternal life (see John 10:10). For Christians, faith is rooted in the encounter with a person, Jesus Christ. He constitutes the means, the content, and the goal of our destiny. There is no other path, no other truth, no other desire.

Meditation: Reflect on what Jesus really means to you. Do you feel you have a personal relationship with him? How have you seen the Father through Jesus?

Prayer: Most loving Father, you have made your Son the Way, the Truth, and the Life, and you have sent him to us to show us how to seek and find you. Open our eyes to behold this profound truth and give us the grace to follow your Son in all that he has taught.

—Ronald Witherup, PSS

Seeing and Believing

Readings: Acts 13:44-52; John 14:7-14

Scripture:
Whoever has seen me has seen the Father. (John 14:9)

Reflection: People from Missouri allegedly possess a strong streak of skepticism. They come from the Show-Me State. While the origin of the nickname is obscure, it is often taken to mean that they need to see for themselves in order to believe. Although I do not hail from Missouri, I can identify with their attitude. Sometimes I won't accept at face value an affirmation unless I see some proof. In the context of our society's struggles with controversies over fake news, people are becoming less and less accepting of claims without supporting concrete evidence. And even then, some won't believe the facts!

From our perspective centuries later, we might be astonished to think that Philip, as recounted in today's gospel, would not know Jesus' identity and his origin from the Father after having spent so much time with him. Yet who would have believed that the God of all creation, the God who created the universe, would take on flesh, become one like us, and dwell in our midst? We should not be too hard on Philip. We might think we would have known Jesus right away by just *seeing* him, but I doubt it. People often see what they want to see rather than what is right in front of them.

Meditation: Everyone has "blind spots," areas where we do not perceive our own weaknesses or the truth of a situation that confronts us. How can we open ourselves up to a larger perspective? What holds you back from perceiving the risen Jesus working in your life? Ask the Lord to give you *in*sight.

Prayer: Lord Jesus, you have revealed to us your heavenly Father and have shared with us that intimacy that exists between you. We sometimes fail to perceive the truth of your revelation, yet we also profess our faith in what you have revealed. Help us in our unbelief, Lord, and don't hold against us our moments of skepticism.

—Ronald Witherup, PSS

New Creation

Readings: Acts 14:21-27; Rev 21:1-5a; John 13:31-33a, 34-35

Scripture:
Then I, John, saw a new heaven and a new earth.
The former heaven and earth had passed away,
    and the sea was no more. . . .

The One who sat on the throne said,
    "Behold, I make all things new." (Rev 21:1, 5a)

Reflection: My car is more than twenty years old. It still runs well most of the time, though little by little parts have had to be replaced, and the body is showing its age. I am getting excited planning to buy a new car—something with that "new car" smell.

In our "throwaway" culture of planned obsolescence, we place a high value on newness. We want the latest technology, the newest gizmos with fancy features, and the latest styles. Who doesn't like new *things*?

But what does it mean for God to promise a *new creation*? How can the entire creation be made new? The whole Bible, in fact, expresses this hope. Throughout the Easter season, we have also been celebrating this desire, which has already begun through the resurrection of the Lord Jesus himself, the "firstborn" of the new creation. The vision of John of Patmos, narrated in the second reading today, speaks of "a new heaven and a new earth," as well as a "new Jerusalem," a re-created holy city where God will dwell anew with the human race and all will be at peace.

As we move further into the twenty-first century, it is more and more apparent that the need for a new earth may not simply be a metaphorical desire. As Pope Francis pointed out in his encyclical letter *Laudato Sì*, we are polluting our land, seas, and air at unprecedented rates. Unlike a car, we cannot simply trade in our planet for a new one. This is our "common home," and we have to take care of it for the long haul. Even while we await the fulfillment of the biblical vision of a new creation where all will dwell in harmony, we must wrestle with how to make that vision present here and now by caring for the planet in better ways.

Meditation: Reflect on your own pattern of care for earthly things. Can you improve on your own use of created goods? Concretely, what can you, your family, your community, or your parish do to better care for our precious planet?

Prayer: Gracious God, Creator of the universe and sustainer of all life, we implore your blessing upon us and our fragile planet that we have not always cared for as good stewards. Bear patiently with us as we seek to do your will in righteousness and justice, and as we await the coming of your kingdom.

—Ronald Witherup, PSS

Tangible Signs of God's Life

Readings: Acts 14:5-18; John 14:21-26

Scripture:
In bestowing his goodness,
he did not leave himself without witness,
for he gave you rains from heaven and fruitful seasons,
and filled you with nourishment and gladness for your
    hearts. (Acts 14:17)

Reflection: "We could use some good old-fashioned miracles right now." Those are the words of my own faith-filled mother who hopes that if God would just "wow" us as in the early days of the church, we might see more people surrender to God's love and power. It is a noble hope, based in care and love for so many people who seem to have lost their moral compass or given in to despair.

Today's reading from the Acts of the Apostles reminds us that God has been "wowing" us for millennia—in miraculous healings, yes, but also in teaching that nourishes us and in a sacramental awareness of the world around us.

In our reading from Acts, the very fruitfulness of nature testifies to the Creator, whose will is to be recognized and known. The author of Wisdom (13:1-9), echoed by Paul in Romans 1:19-21, says those who are ignorant of God have foolishly ignored the evidence of nature, having failed to recognize the artisan of all that is. A cloud-filled valley and a striking sunset have the power to speak to us of God, as does a volcano or a consuming fire.

All manner of nature reveals something of this God who has the power to bring life out of death. In the early church, those who testified to the Good News saw the resurrection of Jesus as the ultimate extension of the Creator's will for life. That's cause for amazement, yes, but it's more. Such awe allows us to see that God dwells with us.

Meditation: In the Northern Hemisphere, the Easter season corresponds with the emergence of color and the evidence of new life. Nature itself is on display in a riot of growth, and its testimony is hard to miss. What evidence do you find in your field of vision right at this moment that gladdens your heart? What shards of color and brilliance not only grab your attention but become an invitation to encounter the God who authors and restores life?

Prayer: O God of all that is, you gladden our hearts with beauty and fill us with the nourishment we need to live each day. In this season of new life, help us to be witnesses to your loving care and your abiding presence.

—Catherine Upchurch

The Work of Evangelization

Readings: Acts 14:19-28; John 14:27-31a

Scripture:
They traveled, . . . they went down, . . . they sailed, . . .
they arrived, . . . they spent no little time with the disciples.
(Acts 14:24-28)

Reflection: The disciples of Jesus strapped on their sandals
and got to work; there was a great big world in need of the
Gospel. Equipped with the Spirit of God and a sense of urgency, those who knew Jesus best did the amazing work of
growing the church all over the Roman Empire in a relatively
brief time. The cascading use of verbs (which we learned in
school are "action words") in just a short portion from Acts
reminds us that the work of evangelization was, and is, about
taking action!

It's not hard to imagine how we might feel if we were
locked in a room in the middle of a city where our leader
was put to death just a few days earlier—fearful, confused,
abandoned, and worried. It's also not hard to imagine that
if that same leader showed up fresh from the grave and fully
alive, we would do whatever he asks of us. We would tap
into the courage, wisdom, and passion that he sent with the
gift of his own Spirit. We'd want to heal and teach and encourage just as he did. And we'd get busy.

All these centuries later, we have our own experiences of encounter with the risen Lord. Perhaps this happens through the sacraments, sacred reading, blessed friendships, or even pain or illness. We too have been given the Spirit and a job description. It's our turn to go, to witness, to spend time, and any other verb we might imagine that puts us to work in the kingdom.

Meditation: If you could describe your particular work of evangelization, large or small, what verbs would you use? How do your actions give witness to the risen Lord? And in what ways do you balance your sacred comings and goings with simply being with and learning from others who know the Lord? And in being with the Lord himself in quiet and prayer?

Prayer: Bless our feet, loving Lord, so that our steps will follow your lead and our arrivals will bring the Good News. Thank you for the grace-filled opportunities in this Easter season to bear witness to the power of life over death.

—Catherine Upchurch

May 22: Wednesday of the Fifth Week of Easter

Tempered by God's Grace

Readings: Acts 15:1-6; John 15:1-8

Scripture:
Just as a branch cannot bear fruit on its own
　unless it remains on the vine,
　　so neither can you unless you remain in me. (John 15:4)

Reflection: Many of us in the Western world, and in developed regions in particular, tend to imagine that we operate pretty independently. We still picture that symbolic bootstrap, and, in our mind's eye, we are pulling it up with our own two hands. We may have bought into the delusion that, since we can accomplish so much on our own, we can even manage spiritual enlightenment or salvation or fullness of life on our own as well.

Today's gospel reminds us that none of that is true. We do not operate independently. If our "bootstraps" have been pulled up, we surely had assistance, and we cannot accomplish anything of spiritual significance under our own steam. It's all grace, that undeserved gift of God's very self that allows us to bear fruit. The opportunities we are given and the accomplishments others may notice are reminders that we operate within the vineyard that God has planted, attached to the vine for sustenance. Even the very soil is divine gift.

To remain in Jesus, as a branch remains on the vine, is to dwell with or to abide with him. It is to acknowledge our need for this intimate connection with Jesus that is permanent and productive. Our ability to love, to speak truth, to respond to needs, to accomplish great things for the kingdom—all of it—depends on an awareness that we cannot do it alone. Our very self depends on remaining in Jesus.

Meditation: In his letter to the Galatians (5:22), Paul also talks about fruitfulness and describes it as "love, joy, peace, patience, kindness, generosity, faithfulness, gentleness, self-control." Likewise the first chapter of First Peter outlines what could be counted as fruit in Christian living: virtue, knowledge, devotion, mutual affection, and love. Spend some quiet time sorting through the fruit of your life and asking for the grace to remain connected to the vine that is Jesus.

Prayer: Temper our self-reliance, dear Jesus, with the knowledge that you were totally dependent on your Father. Help us to model our life on the image of the branch that bears fruit only when attached to the vine.

—Catherine Upchurch

Making Room for God

Readings: Acts 15:7-21; John 15:9-11

Scripture:
God, who knows the heart,
   bore witness by granting them the Holy Spirit
   just as he did us. (Acts 15:8)

Reflection: Creating a space for something new in an already crowded place takes equal parts imagination and rejection. We have to have a vision for where this new item belongs, and we have to be willing to throw out some other items that stand in the way of achieving our goal. We are able to let go of the old if we recognize that what is new has meaning and purpose for us.

Today's reading from Acts is about creating space, a space for God to work in new ways. The predominately Jewish early church finds itself facing the reality that Gentiles are hearing the Good News and responding in faith. Creating a place for them in the church means acknowledging that God is doing something unexpected. God is working outside of the normal avenues of the Mosaic covenant. Will the church respond by letting go of some of the former assumptions to make room for this new work of God? To make room for the changing face of God's people?

This critical decision in the early church reminds us that God cannot be restrained by our limited understandings. But this is not just a lesson in usually divine unpredictability; it is a reminder that God *is* predictable in knowing the human heart. The hearts of Gentiles have turned to Jesus, and the hearts of the first believers would widen to accept them.

Meditation: Centuries ago, the prophet proclaimed that God's ways are not our ways (Isa 55:8-9). We tend to think and act within the confines of what is comfortable to us, to read and listen to what confirms our already firm view of the world. We tend to expect God to act within these same parameters. Reflect on how the Easter season, with its stories of the emerging communities of faith in Acts, can remind you that God may lead you into new territories and will no doubt broaden your heart in the process.

Prayer: With St. Augustine, we call out to you, "O Beauty ever ancient, ever new." Give us the wisdom to discover the constancy of your work in our hearts and the courage to allow you to break through our deafness and shine through our blindness. Do a new work in us, O God.

—Catherine Upchurch

The Company We Keep

Readings: Acts 15:22-31; John 15:12-17

Scripture:
No one has greater love than this,
   to lay down one's life for one's friends. (John 15:13)

Reflection: "You can judge a person's character by the company he or she keeps." This popular adage is usually employed to encourage our children to select good friends, to determine for ourselves who will receive our business, or even to evaluate political candidates. It is a practical piece of wisdom that gets turned on its head in the life and ministry of Jesus.

Part of human development from a young age is determining who is "in" and who is "out," who is acceptable and who is not. In New Testament times, this was amplified by a system of honor and shame, where one avoided associations and circumstances that might dishonor one's family or oneself. Jesus' interactions in his public ministry demonstrate that he is not concerned with such categories or social taboos. He scandalizes his contemporaries by counting the unwashed, the broken, and many outliers among his friends. Jesus even loves these friends so much that he gives his life for them and in the process offers them, us, fullness of life.

The company Jesus keeps tells us that he is more concerned with relationships than with appearances, more oriented to service than to social standing, and more committed to revealing God than to controlling access to God. He would rather embrace the unclean than preserve his ritual purity. He would rather truly love than ignore the lost. The Easter message is that, in choosing us, he asks us to do the same.

Meditation: When we confess that Jesus came to save the lost, to heal the sick, and to embrace the sinner, do we count ourselves among them? Do we long for the friendship that Jesus offers so freely? The Gospel of John makes clear that such friendship brings light to a world in darkness and life where death might appear to hold sway. Thus is the power of God's love poured out in Christ.

Prayer: O God of life, remind us in these resurrection days that our task is to love as you love and to keep company with those who will most benefit from the gift of your love. Make it possible for us to lay down our lives in practical ways and in ordinary places.

—Catherine Upchurch

Behind the Numbers

Readings: Acts 16:1-10; John 15:18-21

Scripture:
Day after day the churches grew stronger in faith
   and increased in number. (Acts 16:5)

Reflection: We live in a world saturated in numbers—the stock market, grocery store prices, scores in sports, business spreadsheets, class grades, reported attendees at an event, and many other examples. Sometimes we even obsess about numbers, wanting high scores on class tests, large numbers in seminaries, and smaller numbers when we step on the scales. We gauge the health of our economy on quarterly reports that involve more numbers: unemployment and inflation rates, the national debt, interest rates, and average wages.

And now, in the Acts of the Apostles, we discover what seems to be a modern theme. The church's growth is measured in the numbers of those being saved and joining the community of believers. We can hardly imagine what it might have meant to be part of this fledgling community of believers who meet without benefit of public buildings and espouse a leader who died an inglorious death. The surrounding culture knows little of Christian beliefs and practices and certainly would not adopt many of their values.

That there is growth at all is a testament to the power of the Spirit and the nature of the early church's witness.

This growth in faith and in numbers is noticed "day by day," person by person. Behind the numbers are real wives and husbands, day laborers and vineyard owners, shepherds and scribes, soldiers and merchants, and surely plenty of widows and orphans. The church may have increased in numbers but its growth in maturity happened through individuals who lived in community.

Meditation: When we watch people come forward to receive the Eucharist, we see all kinds of hands—rough, manicured, wrinkled, chubby, gentle, and strong. These are the hands of the individuals who make up the numbers we report in our parishes. Contemplate how the daily work of these hands is part of the building up of the Body of Christ.

Prayer: Spirit of God, stir within us true growth in faith. May our increase in numbers never outpace our growth in the kind of faith that puts complete trust in God. And when our numbers wane, give us the desire to bear effective witness to what is true and good in this world, and the strength to continue building.

—Catherine Upchurch

There Is No Fear in Love

Readings: Acts 15:1-2, 22-29; Rev 21:10-14, 22-23; John 14:23-29

Scripture:
Do not let your hearts be troubled or afraid. (John 14:25)

Reflection: At this point in the story line of John's gospel, the followers of Jesus could not have known the full horror of what awaited Jesus in Jerusalem. Nor would they have known that the grave he would occupy would become the cradle of new life. But the evangelist writing the gospel a few decades after the events knew it full well. By accenting these assurances from Jesus at this point, John is making sure that in his narrative the light of the resurrection outshines the shadow of the cross.

There is plenty to trouble hearts and cause anxiety. Roman soldiers are occupying Israel in this first-century period. Jewish factions are promoting various responses to this foreign occupation. Jesus' own words and actions put him at odds with both the political and religious leaders of his own people. And yet those who follow Jesus are to quiet their hearts and have no fear.

Jesus calls for a type of trust that is absolute. It begins by acknowledging that, although we have fears and limitations, we are not defined by them. Ultimately, such trust is surrendering to the one who cries out for the cup of suffering to be removed, the one who calls out to his Father when he feels abandoned, the one who, in the end, trusts in God's power to bring life from death. This is the truth of Easter.

Meditation: Part of the human condition is dealing with troubling situations of all kinds. People of faith are not exempt from personal disasters, insecurity about the future, or concern for family members. Our defense is to trust in the God whose love emptied the tomb. The First Letter of John (4:18) is a reminder that there is no fear in love, and that perfect love casts out fear. As you grow in love, fear diminishes.

Prayer: This day we pray, O God of Love, for the shadow of the cross to diminish as the light of Easter fills the universe. May this same light shine in our hearts so that our thoughts and actions deepen our trust in you. Calm our hearts and strengthen us in love to help carry the world's troubles.

—Catherine Upchurch

Lydia

Readings: Acts 16:11-15; John 15:26–16:4a

Scripture:
. . . a woman named Lydia, a dealer in purple cloth,
   from the city of Thyatira, a worshiper of God, listened,
   and the Lord opened her heart to pay attention
   to what Paul was saying. (Acts 16:14)

Reflection: In the Greek city of Philippi, Paul, Silas, and Luke meet Lydia. In a society where it was rare for a woman to both head a household and manage a business, Lydia has done very well dealing in "purple cloth," a luxurious fabric purchased by the wealthy. Though not a Jew herself, Lydia worships the God of Judaism and respects the rituals and customs of the Jewish faith. Paul's words profoundly move Lydia and she and her household are baptized. Lydia offers Paul and Luke the hospitality of her home: Lydia's house becomes the meeting place for the newly formed Christian community in Philippi—her home may well be the first Christian church in Europe.

Lydia bears the responsibilities of caring for her family and household, of managing the many details of her business, of keeping ahead of the demands of the marketplace. While struggling to make a living, Lydia wants to live a life of meaning. Amid all these challenges and responsibilities,

Lydia sees herself as part of something greater than herself and seeks to understand the meaning of her role in that "something." It is that seeking that opens her heart to the Gospel preached by this Paul.

We can readily see ourselves in Lydia. Like Lydia, we juggle many roles in our lives simultaneously: we are parents, sons and daughters, brothers and sisters; we are managers and workers; we seek to belong, to make our mark, to make a difference. And in all of these roles, we struggle to "pay attention" to the signs of God's love in our midst as we conduct the business of the day and make our homes gathering places of God's peace.

Meditation: How can you integrate the Gospel principles of compassion and justice in the many and different roles you play in your life?

Prayer: Open our hearts, O God, to embrace your Word of peace and compassion, and let that Word resound in the many roles we play, in the many places where we live and work. Come and make our home your dwelling place, where all who come to our table find welcome and peace.

—Jay Cormier

May 28: Tuesday of the Sixth Week of Easter

Released!

Readings: Acts 16:22-34; John 16:5-11

Scripture:
When the jailer woke up and saw the prison doors
    wide open,
  he drew his sword and was about to kill himself,
  thinking that the prisoners had escaped.
But Paul shouted out in a loud voice,
  "Do no harm to yourself; we are all here." (Acts 16:27-28)

Reflection: The perfect escape: an earthquake strikes in the middle of the night, the prison doors collapse, the chains easily come loose from the crumbled walls. All Paul and Silas have to do is slip out in the midst of the chaos.

But they don't.

Paul and Silas know how this would play out: Once they escaped, their jailer would kill himself for letting his prisoners get away (such would be the expectation of his superiors), and a family would be without a husband and father and son and brother. So Paul assures the jailer that he and Silas are still there. The jailer is stunned by such extraordinary compassion and wants to know what kind of God inspires such selfless generosity that enables them to put a poor jailer's life before their own. The jailer encounters God not in a doctrine or teaching but in another's act of uncommon kindness. This is the Spirit, the Advocate, that Jesus promises in today's gospel: God's light that opens our hearts to compassion and empathy, God's grace that frees us from our terrifying prisons of selfishness, arrogance, and bigotry.

Every one of us can do the same: to bring the Gospel of Jesus into the life of others through acts of simple kindness motivated by Christ-like compassion. The most effective "catechism" we can preach is selfless generosity. The Gospel that mirrors the servanthood of Christ Jesus is most powerfully revealed in humble service to others; the love of God is experienced in the mercy and forgiveness that we extend to one another and that we humbly accept from others.

Meditation: Is there some situation you are currently dealing with that you can transform into something good or positive by putting your interests second for the sake of another?

Prayer: Father of reconciliation and forgiveness, help us to honor your presence within the heart of every man, woman, and child. May we seek their good before our own; may we take the first step to crossing the chasms that divide us; may we reveal your love in our care and welcome to them.

—Jay Cormier

Our Altars to "Unknown Gods"

Readings: Acts 17:15, 22–18:1; John 16:12-15

Scripture:
For as I walked around looking carefully at your shrines,
   I even discovered an altar inscribed "To an Unknown
   God."
What therefore you unknowingly worship, I proclaim to
   you. (Acts 17:23)

Reflection: Paul and his traveling companions have arrived at Athens, the ancient capital of Greek government, commerce, and philosophy. Here they see the many shrines and altars dedicated to the icons of Greek philosophy and culture and the many gods of Greek mythology. One shrine celebrates the work ethic espoused by Epicurus; another altar honors the Stoic god of reason who governed the cosmos. Paul even comes to an altar erected "To an Unknown God." This "Unknown God" serves as the starting point for Paul's introduction of the God revealed by Christ in the gospels.

In our own lives, in our own "Athens," we have built altars dedicated to unknown gods who have more influence on our decisions and relationships than we realize:

The God of Ambition, to whom we offer all our time and energy in pursuit of wealth and recognition.

The God of the Biggest, whom we honor by never being satisfied with anything less than the newest, the coolest, the biggest, the best.

The God of Winning, to whom we sacrifice our very humanity to win at all costs, whether at business, on the playing field, in politics.

The God of Instant Gratification, to whom we seek our own pleasure and profit before all else.

The God of Me, in whom we see ourselves as the center of all things.

During this Easter season consider the gods we worship with our time, attention, and energy. Look at the shrines we have built to them—and see how empty they are.

Meditation: What values do you spend your time and energy pursuing? What sacrifices do you make to these gods? How can you make this Easter a time for rediscovering the grace of God "in whom we live and move and have our being"?

Prayer: May every encounter and work of our lives be an offering of grateful praise for your many blessings, O God. May our homes and work spaces, our calendars and planners, our hearts and spirits, become shrines of your loving presence in our lives and the lives of those we love.

—Jay Cormier

"A Little While . . ."

Readings: Acts 18:1-8; John 16:16-20

Scripture:
A little while and you will no longer see me,
    and again a little while later and you will see me.
    (John 16:16)

Reflection: "A little while" can be a long time.

"A little while" can be a long, dark night of fear and despair.

"A little while" can be an endless struggle to put back together the pieces of the broken relationship or mend the shattered heart.

Our lives are a constant turning over of "little whiles": the relationship that sours, the promise that is never fulfilled, the obstacle that we can't find a way around.

Jesus' concept of "little whiles" challenges our understanding of time. Time is both our most precious possession and our most feared enemy. We suffer a small death with every "little while" of waiting and hoping.

"A little while" is one of those markers in the gospel that reminds us that all time is a gift from God. In God's scheme of things, our lives are "a little while," a "brief candle" that burns brightly for an instant. The light that illuminates our way through all of these "little whiles" is the hope of the

Easter Christ. That "light" may be the loved one or friend who stayed with us through that difficult night, who called and let us safely vent our frustration and outrage, whose thoughtfulness assured us that we were not alone.

Jesus asks us to trust the Father as he trusted the Father: that God is *with* us in our grief and sadness and that God is *in* us when we are able to bring light and joy into the lives of those mired in hurt and brokenness.

In the gospel, we learn the patience needed to move from "a little while" to fulfillment of Easter hope.

It just may take "a little while."

Meditation: What anxious "little while" are you currently experiencing and what will the fulfillment of that "little while" look like?

Prayer: May we place our trust in you, O God, never forgetting the many ways in which we realize your wisdom, compassion, and forgiveness in our midst. Help us to treat every moment of our lives as sacred and holy and to see every step we walk as a part of our lifelong journey to your dwelling place.

—Jay Cormier

To the Marys and Elizabeths in Our Lives

Readings: Zeph 3:14-18a or Rom 12:9-16; Luke 1:39-56

Scripture:
Mary set out
   and traveled to the hill country in haste
   to a town of Judah,
   where she entered the house of Zechariah
   and greeted Elizabeth. (Luke 1:39-40)

Reflection: Today's feast celebrates two extraordinary women: Mary, the pregnant unmarried teenager, still reeling from her situation, who rushes to be with her beloved kin in her hour of need; and the elder (and miraculously pregnant) Elizabeth, whose joy and faith become a source of reassurance to her young, overwhelmed, pregnant cousin. Together they prepare for the difficult roles God has called them to take on.

Most of us are blessed to have a "Mary" in our lives: the family member or friend who is the first one there when there is crisis, the first one who calls to ask what she can do to help, the first one we turn to when we need a listening ear.

And most families have a cherished "Elizabeth" in their midst: the wise grandmother or grandfather, the beloved aunt or uncle who has seen it all and instinctively knows the right thing to do or say; the older brother or sister who tells you the straight, unvarnished truth because he or she has been there and has made that same mistake or faced that same set of circumstances; the friend who has stuck by you, and you with them, through hard times and long nights.

Today, may we give thanks for "the visitation" moments that have graced all of our lives and remember in grateful prayer the Marys and Elizabeths among us—and may we possess the selflessness and generosity of heart to be a Mary of support and help or an Elizabeth of wisdom and grace for someone we love.

Meditation: Who are the Mary and Elizabeth in your life—and how might you be a Mary or Elizabeth to a loved one or friend in need?

Prayer: Gracious God, instill in us your Spirit, that we may become sisters and mothers, brothers and fathers to one another as Mary and Elizabeth were for each other. May your love be the heart of our family and community that always brings us together; may Mary's song of fearless hope and persevering joy become our song of joy and hope in the promise of your mercy.

—Jay Cormier

Praying for the "Right" Thing

Readings: Acts 18:23-28; John 16:23b-28

Scripture:
Amen, amen, I say to you,
whatever you ask the Father in my name he will give
you. (John 16:23b)

Reflection: We've all asked God for something—in Jesus' name even. No go.

We've cajoled, pleaded, even promised to sacrifice. *Still waiting, God.*

We've even tried going through his mother, Mary. Nothing.

And most of the time, we're not even asking for ourselves: good lab test results for her, a job offer for him, a successful fundraising campaign for the church. *Hello, God, are you there?*

So what's the point of prayer?

Maybe what is "off" is our expectations of prayer. In his book *Nine Essential Things I've Learned about Life*, Rabbi Harold Kushner writes: "It isn't God's job to make sick people healthy. That's the doctors' job. God's job is to make sick people brave, and in my experience, that's something God does very well. [Prayer] is not a matter of begging or bargaining. It is the act of inviting God into our lives so that, with God's help, we will be strong enough to resist temptation and resilient enough not to be destroyed by life's unfairness."

Rabbi Kushner makes two important points: First, prayer is about seeking to do what *God* asks of us—not God doing what *we* want God to do. Prayer is to seek the courage to deal with the difficult illness, the patience to save the relationship that is faltering, the wisdom to transform our poverty into blessing. Second, the very act of prayer is to "invite" God into the joys and struggles of our lives, to be aware of God's constant presence in every moment of our lives.

In these last days of Easter, may we reconsider what we seek from God and refocus our prayer on realizing God's grace in our lives, enabling us to face the challenges of our lives with a spirit of gratitude and an attitude of hope.

Meditation: What are you currently seeking of God in prayer—and are you sure you are asking for the "right" thing?

Prayer: Illuminate our lives in every season, O God, with the light of Easter joy. May our prayers seek not things but grace. May our joy be complete not in what we gain but in what we give. May what we ask in your Son's name be worthy of his name.

—Jay Cormier

Sacred Trust

Readings: Acts 1:1-11; Eph 1:17-23 or Heb 9:24-28; 10:19-23; Luke 24:46-53

Scripture:
You are witnesses of these things.
And behold I am sending the promise of my Father upon you. (Luke 24:48-49a)

Reflection: We entrust significant parts of our lives to professionals who win our confidence by their competence and skill. We entrust the care and education of our children to teachers and coaches. We entrust our retirement investments and children's college funds to financial managers. We entrust the structural integrity of our homes to contractors, electricians, and plumbers. We entrust our safety and health to firefighters, police, doctors, and nurses.

Likewise, we are entrusted with the interests of our employers, our clients, our friends, and, most important of all, of our children and families.

To entrust some part of our lives to another requires our letting go, respecting their expertise and experience, and accepting the reality that change is both difficult and inevitable, as well as unpredictable. And to accept the responsibility of another's trust requires us to put aside our own interests to seek what is best for those who have placed their confidence in us. Such trust is sacred.

Today, on the mount of the Ascension, Jesus entrusts to his remnant of followers his Gospel of healing, compassion, reconciliation, and hope. Having given his life to revealing God's love for all humankind, he entrusts that work to us and every disciple of every time and place. He commissions us to be his witnesses and so continue his work, with all its risks and despite all our doubts. To build Christ's church requires from us humility, respect, patience; the Risen One's trust compels us to let go of our own interests in order to open our hearts to change and the costs of such change.

In our quietest, simplest, and most ordinary expressions of compassion and care, we keep faith with the trust of the Risen One: to be his witnesses to his life, death, and resurrection in our own Jerusalems and beyond.

Meditation: What obstacles do you experience in trusting the promises of the Gospel of the Risen Christ?

Prayer: O Lord, make us worthy and effective witnesses of the Gospel you have entrusted to us. Illuminate our works of compassion and ministries of care with the light of Easter hope. May your grace enable us to trust in our own abilities to reveal your constant love in the midst of our families and communities.

—Jay Cormier

June 3: Saint Charles Lwanga and Companions, Martyrs

In Other Words

Readings: Acts 19:1-8; John 16:29-33

Scripture:
Now you are talking plainly. (John 16:29)

Reflection: "Proclaim the good news!" says Jesus to his followers. We'll see them spilling out into the streets to do just that next Sunday. Proclaim! Preach! A small voice protests from the back of the room. "Not me! I'm just a pew person. I never studied any theology. I can't preach!"

St. Charles Lwanga and his companions would beg to differ. They were just pew people too, but in the court of the Ugandan king they served. They gave no sermons, but they preached as St. Francis is reputed to have taught his followers: "Preach the Gospel! Use words if you have to." They preached the Gospel in plain language by living it, and at great cost. They rebuked the king for the murderous, debauched life he led, and they refused to accede to his demands to join in. This was a message the king could not misunderstand but would not accept. So he ordered their execution. The youngest of them was only thirteen.

Announcing the Gospel from a pulpit or teacher's desk or even a street corner may be beyond our calling and skill, but living it is not. Wherever we are, whatever we're doing, whatever the price tag, we have been strengthened by the

Spirit to live the life of Christ into which we were baptized. No ordination required. No academic study necessary. All we need to learn and live this language is willingness, integrity, prayer, and, now and then, the courage that is one of the Spirit's gifts.

Meditation: Can you remember persons whose Gospel integrity inspired you to understand and live the Gospel better? How? Can you remember times when your commitment to living the Gospel was challenged? How did you respond? If you caved to the language of a world apparently untouched by the Good News, just turn to St. Peter for help. He knows all about unfaithfulness and forgiveness.

Prayer: O Jesus, Word of God made flesh, steep me more and more in the language of love you proclaimed and lived, and keep me faithful to it when challenges come.

—Genevieve Glen, OSB

June 4: Tuesday of the Seventh Week of Easter

What Then?

Readings: Acts 20:17-27; John 17:1-11a

Scripture:
Now this is eternal life,
   that they should know you, the only true God,
   and the one whom you have sent, Jesus Christ.
      (John 17:3)

Reflection: Somehow we've always wanted someone to come back from the dead and tell us what life is like after death. And in this Easter season we rejoice that someone has. The risen Christ is of course disappointingly silent about the things we want to know, beyond the huge fact that there really *is* life after death. But in fact, in his last instruction to his disciples on the eve of his own death, he did tell us exactly what we need to know: eternal life is knowing God.

What about the details? What will we look like? What will we do? Surely not just strum harps all the time! But wait: there *is* no time after death!

Jesus gives us the heart of the matter. The details will have to wait. Doing, achieving, acquiring—all those words will fall away, hard as it seems to us to let them go. Eternal life is knowing the Father and the Word made flesh. (Jesus speaks of Spirit elsewhere). You've heard, I'm sure, that biblical knowing is not the mind acquiring facts. It is entering into a communion with another that is profound beyond words. The best the biblical world can do for an example is the mutual self-giving in an ideal sexual union. On this side of the grave, in a world still riddled with sin, we can't imagine that any more than we can imagine life without time.

But we have foretastes. A true friendship or marriage that grows from depth to depth, an experience of Christ in word, sacrament, and community that draws us more and more out of our selfishness into mutual love: those are previews that must keep us going until we get there. And they are our responsibilities now.

Meditation: What are your deepest relationships? Can you imagine them growing into the kind of communion in Christ that Paul's image of the Body of Christ describes? What can you do—or stop doing—to move toward that? Are you willing to know and be known at that depth? If not, why not? What are you afraid of?

Prayer: O God, free me from all that holds me back from becoming one in truth and love with you in Christ's living Body.

—Genevieve Glen, OSB

Beware of Wolves!

Readings: Acts 20:28-38; John 17:11b-19

Scripture:
I am coming to you. . . .
As you sent me into the world,
   so I sent them into the world. (John 17:13, 18)

Reflection: Psalm 23 is my favorite. After leaving the green oasis and passing through the dark valley, who can't feel relief at being seated at the table the Lord has prepared? But one day I noticed the next line: "in the sight of my enemies." I suddenly realized that the Lord's table isn't safely ensconced within the stout walls of God's house. It seems to sit in a clearing at whose edges wolves are prowling. The One who is Light of the World presides at table and deters them for now. But after the meal, we still have a ways to go, with "goodness and mercy following," before we reach the house of the Lord. That's the road we're on.

So were Jesus' followers at the Last Supper table, and so were Paul's at his last meal with them in Ephesus. As Jesus and Paul both say goodbye, they pray for those they leave behind. Jesus prays for their protection against the Evil One, the Devourer paradoxically defeated but not yet destroyed by the cross. Jesus sets joy and truth as their armor. Paul warns that wolves will fall on the flock even from within their own ranks, wielding the weapons of untruth and division.

So let's not take our Easter "alleluia" as a melodic sigh of relief. Despite the familiar hymn, the strife isn't over yet. We're in the thick of it. Jesus' resurrection broke the ultimate hold of sin and death, those long-toothed wolves, but as a beginning and promise to sustain us on the road. "Alleluia," with its overtones of joy and truth, is the shield and battle song we take up together for the long march, not our final Amen. St. Augustine calls it our traveling song.

Meditation: What are the wolves that threaten you on the road? Fear? Fatigue? Discouragement? Name them: coming out into the light warns them off. And remember, even the fiercest of wolves can't triumph over resurrection joy and truth. So put yourself in the Shepherd's care and refuse whatever the red-eyed prowlers would use to weaken and scatter. Sing faith's "alleluia!" and travel on.

Prayer: O Christ, good Shepherd, protect me on the way as I walk with you into God's reign.

—Genevieve Glen, OSB

June 6: Thursday of the Seventh Week of Easter

Watchmaker at Work

Readings: Acts 22:30; 23:6-11; John 17:20-26

Scripture:
. . . that they may be one, as we are one. (John 17:22)

Reflection: Over the past few years, our monastic community has been watching videos exploring the wonders of creation and creativity, from Madagascar's elusive animals to Monet's waterlilies, from the delicate stone lace in underground caverns to Bach's music and Shakespeare's poetry. I keep thinking of a watchmaker with apprentices: God and God's human images putting large and small working pieces of reality into a universe that moves with the intricate precision of the Switzerland's jeweled timepieces.

How grieved the divine Watchmaker must have been to see a destructive fist smash the interlocking movements to pieces when the first human beings tore up the design and put their tools to use to build a world of "me first." Of course, they didn't understand any more than we do that taking care of number one breaks all the little springs and wheels of God's design into social and ecological chaos. Down the countless millennia since, the Watchmaker has worked tirelessly with new generations of apprentices to put the pieces back together. In the risen Christ, the work succeeds.

Jesus' prayer that all may be one after the pattern of the Trinity has the anguished urgency of the primal Watchmaker reaching out for the pieces of a broken world and preparing to shed blood to mend it. We are the present generation of apprentices. We could quit the job as our forebears did. We could stand back and watch the work go on as if it were just a video. But we've been warned: the Spirit whose coming we soon celebrate will blow us, like the disciples, out of our comfort zones into the streets to gather up whatever pieces of Eden's wreckage we can reach—because there are survivors there crying for our help. And sometimes we ourselves are they.

Meditation: The everyday chaos around us unfortunately seems normal, but the breakages are real. And we have made some of them ourselves. What is one practical thing you could do to pick up pieces and put them back together?

Prayer: O Christ, the heart of the world made one, enlighten me and strengthen me to work for the unity you desire.

—Genevieve Glen, OSB

Take and Eat!

Readings: Acts 25:13b-21; John 21:15-19

Scripture:
Feed my sheep. (John 21:17)

Reflection: Imagine: you've just put your all into preparing a nourishing meal, and almost no one eats. One won't leave a video game, another is chasing sales at the mall, yet another wants only potato chips or dessert. Just a few sit down to eat the meal—and thank you for it. How do you feel?

Not all of us are called to serve as shepherds charged with feeding Jesus' flock, but buried in Jesus' instructions to Peter to do just that is Jesus' deep desire for the flock to eat what is set before us. Peter knows perfectly well what that is. He has seen this Good Shepherd take a few loaves and feed thousands with lots of leftovers. He was there when Jesus took the festive Passover bread, blessed, broke, and passed it around the table, saying: "Take and eat; this is my body" (Matt 26:26). Actions speak louder than words, it's true, but before serving the bread on both of these occasions, Jesus served up a hefty course of words. They weren't just any words, idle chatter to break the ice and pass the time. They were life-defining and life-changing words. The subtext was clear: "You're hungry for a life that has meaning; you're hungry to become something more; you're hungry for the communion with God you may not even be able to name. Take in these words, make them your own, and you will become all that you desire to be, and more."

And Bread and Word are both offered to us now, in generous helpings—the Bread at Mass, and the Word sitting right there in our Bibles. Jesus still literally puts his all into this feast for the beloved flock: take and eat!

Meditation: Jesus doesn't expect us to be at Mass or immersed in our Bibles 24/7, but it's all too easy to choose junk food for the soul before prayer in word and sacrament. And junk food easily becomes habit. What's on your menu?

Prayer: Jesus, Word and Bread of Life, draw us deeper into the feast you set before us in liturgy and Scripture so that we might grow more and more like you who prepare and serve us your very self in love.

—Genevieve Glen, OSB

Cliffhangers

Readings: Acts 28:16-20, 30-31; John 21:20-25

Scripture:
What if I want [the Beloved Disciple] to remain until I come? What concern is it of yours? You follow me. (John 21:22)

Reflection: Don't you hate it when a TV season's closing or a novel's ending leaves us asking, "What then?" Narrative curiosity doesn't like to be thwarted by unfinished stories.

Yet here on the brink of Pentecost we learn that the stories we've been following don't end here. As Acts closes, Paul remains under house arrest in Rome. What happens next? Tradition recounts Paul's death, but Luke doesn't even mention it. As John's gospel ends, Jesus asks a nosy Peter, "What if I want [the Beloved Disciple] to remain till I come? What business is it of yours? You follow me." What happens next?

Pentecost is not the end of any tale. It's the beginning of the church's story, and that's not over yet. It's the beginning of all our stories as believers infused with the Spirit at baptism, and none of those have ended yet. The present always comes with an edge: the edge where today will slip into tomorrow. What will happen then?

Jesus' answer to Peter served him and us: Never mind what's going to happen to anyone, even you. Your life is now, not tomorrow or next week. Now the only business you have is to follow me. Because tomorrow will be made by the choices you make today.

Perhaps we want to know what's coming next because we've learned that surprises aren't always happy, but if we know the end of the story in all its detail, what is the point of reading on or living on? The end of the story is God's surprise. Our job is not to figure it out. It's to follow Jesus every day until we get there. As we do, *we* become what happens next.

Meditation: In your life's story so far, when has God surprised you out of the plot direction you expected and into one unforeseen? How have your own choices led there? How has your story been shaped by following Christ or by choosing not to?

Prayer: O God, Creator and Storyteller, teach me to read your signs as I go so that my story reaches the ending you desire for me.

—Genevieve Glen, OSB

The New Creation: Babel Undone

Readings: Acts 2:1-11; 1 Cor 12:3b-7, 12-13 or Rom 8:8-17; John 20:19-23 or John 14:15-16, 23b-26

Scripture:
[T]hey were all filled with the Holy Spirit
   and began to speak in different tongues . . .
      [but] each one heard them speaking in his own language.
         (Acts 2:4, 6)

Reflection: Striking, isn't it, the role that language plays in the process of creation–uncreation–re-creation we call redemption? In Genesis 1, God uses no tool other than Spirit-born words to draw all things out of the primal chaos. In Genesis 3, the serpent uses clever words to skew the human beings' first choice. In its wake, language—the most human way of bonding us together in mutual understanding—turned adversarial, driving the first couple apart. That original division spreads until, in Genesis 11, the people, still misled by the serpent's subtly setting God and humanity in competition, started to build a tower to reach the heavens—perhaps to seize the divine throne for themselves? God thwarted their plan by wrecking their communication system, confusing their language so they couldn't understand one another and so couldn't cooperate. Hostile, competitive, destructive language remained a hallmark of human interchange ever after.

Until Pentecost. This time, God sent the Spirit to draw all people together by the Gospel preached in languages all hearers could understand. Thus the new creation begins.

We've all had the painful experience of destructive words spoken and bonds of respect, love, and communion broken. It happens at the breakfast table or in the United Nations or at the edges of two ethnic neighborhoods where one group throws verbal sticks and stones at another. And we have learned the hard way that verbal weapons of division, once spoken, can never be taken back. But with the advent of the Spirit, breathed out by Jesus on the cross to bring together what sin had long rent asunder, we can learn a new language. Its most powerful speaker is Jesus, God's own Word made flesh, who spoke, lived, and wielded against human hurt God's creative language of love. Receiving the Spirit, we receive the capacity to mend relationships our own Babels have broken apart. Let's talk to one another!

Meditation: Do you have any relationships that need mending? Receive the Holy Spirit to learn a more loving language.

Prayer: Come, Holy Spirit, and breathe into us God's language of love, that we may reweave lost harmonies and offer one another hope that God's reign will prevail in our world by the power of the risen Word among us.

—Genevieve Glen, OSB

References

April 21: Easter Sunday of the Resurrection of the Lord
Pope Francis, General Audience, April 1, 2015, http://w2.
vatican.va/content/francesco/en/audiences/2015/docu-
ments/papa-francesco_20150401_udienza-generale.html.

April 24: Wednesday within the Octave of Easter
Finbarr G. Clancy, SJ, "St. Augustine's Commentary on the
Emmaus Scene in Luke's Gospel," in *Augustine, Other Latin
Writers, Studia Patristica* 43 (Leuven: Peeters, 2006), 51.

April 25: Thursday within the Octave of Easter
Martin Laird, OSA, *Into the Silent Land: A Guide to the Chris-
tian Practice of Contemplation* (New York: Oxford University
Press, 2006), 79.

April 27: Saturday within the Octave of Easter
David L. Fleming, SJ, *Draw Me into Your Friendship: The Spiri-
tual Exercises, a Literal Translation and a Contemporary Reading*
(St. Louis, MO: The Institute of Jesuit Sources, 1996), 169.

April 28: Second Sunday of Easter
Paul Tillich, *Systematic Theology*, vol. 2 (Chicago: University
of Chicago Press, 1957), 116.

May 7: Tuesday of the Third Week of Easter
John L. Allen Jr., *Shahbaz Bhatti: Martyr of the Suffering Church* (Collegeville, MN: Liturgical Press, 2017), 4, 7.

June 1: Saint Justin, Martyr
Harold S. Kushner, *Nine Essential Things I've Learned about Life* (New York: Alfred A. Knopf, 2015), 28–29.

Contributors

Michelle Francl-Donnay is a writer, teacher, wife, and the mother of two college-aged sons. Her regular column, Catholic Spirituality, appears at the Philadelphia Archdiocese's news site, CatholicPhilly.com. She is a professor of chemistry at Bryn Mawr College and an adjunct scholar of the Vatican Observatory. She blogs about faith and science at http://mfrancldonnay.blogspot.com/ and is a contributor to *Give Us This Day*, and author of *Not by Bread Alone 2018*, published by Liturgical Press.

Jerome Kodell, OSB, is a monk of Subiaco Abbey, where he has honed both his biblical scholarship and his leadership skills as the former abbot. He is a contributor to *Give Us This Day* and the author of several books, including *Twelve Keys to Prayer*; *Don't Trust the Abbot: Musings from the Monastery*; *The Eucharist in the New Testament*; *John the Baptist, Forerunner*; *Barnabas, Man for Others*; and coauthor of *Waiting in Joyful Hope 2015–16* with Genevieve Glen, OSB.

Rachelle Linner, a freelance writer and reviewer, has a master of theological studies from Weston Jesuit School of Theology. She is a librarian by training who recently retired from a career as an editor in software companies. In May 2019 she will complete a two-year Franciscan Spiritual Direction certification program. She is a frequent contributor to *Give Us This Day*.

Ronald D. Witherup, PSS, is superior general of the Sulpicians, an order of diocesan priests dedicated to initial and ongoing formation of priests. He holds a doctorate in biblical studies and is the author of numerous books and articles on Scripture, including *The Word of God at Vatican II: Exploring Dei Verbum* and *Biblical Fundamentalism: What Every Catholic Should Know*, published by Liturgical Press. He is also a contributor to *Give Us This Day*.

Catherine Upchurch serves as the director of Little Rock Scripture Study and the general editor of the *Little Rock Catholic Study Bible*. She brings years of adult faith formation experience to her writing and speaking. She is an associate editor of *The Bible Today*, a regular contributor to *Give Us This Day*, and the author of *Christmas, Season of Wonder and Hope*; *Mary, Favored by God*; *Moses, Called and Equipped*; and *Hospitality, Welcoming the Stranger*.

Jay Cormier is a deacon and editor of Connections, a monthly newsletter for homilists and preachers. He is an adjunct professor of humanities and communications at St. Anselm College in Manchester, New Hampshire, and leads preaching and liturgy workshops for clergy and laity. Cormier has contributed to *America, U.S. Catholic, Worship*, and *Give Us This Day*; and is the author of *The Deacon's Ministry of the Word*, the 2012 and 2013 editions of *Waiting in Joyful Hope*, and previous editions of *Living Liturgy*™ (Liturgical Press).

Genevieve Glen, OSB, is a nun of the contemplative Benedictine monastery of St. Walburga, where she has taught in the formation program and conducted retreats in the retreat house. She has also given retreats in many Benedictine monasteries of women and men. She is a poet, hymn text writer, and essayist who contributes regularly to *Give Us This Day*. She co-authored the 2016 issue of *Waiting in Joyful Hope* with Jerome Kodell, OSB, and is the author of *Not by Bread Alone 2017*, *Waiting in Joyful Hope 2018–19*, and *Sauntering Through Scripture: A Book of Reflections* (2018), published by Liturgical Press.

SEASONAL REFLECTIONS NOW AVAILABLE IN ENGLISH AND SPANISH

ADVENT/ADVIENTO

Waiting in Joyful Hope: Daily Reflections for Advent and Christmas 2019–2020
Daniel G. Groody, CSC

Reflexiones diarias para Adviento y Navidad: Esperando en alegre esperanza 2019–20
Daniel G. Groody, CSC; Translated by Luis Baudry-Simón

LENT/CUARESMA

Not By Bread Alone: Daily Reflections for Lent 2020
Michelle Francl-Donnay

Reflexiones diarias para Cuaresma: No sólo de pan 2020
Michelle Francl-Donnay; Translated by Luis Baudry-Simón

EASTER/PASCUA

Rejoice and Be Glad: Daily Reflections for Easter 2020
Mary DeTurris Poust

Reflexiones diarias para Pascua: Alégrense y regocijense 2020
Mary DeTurris Poust; Translated by Luis Baudry-Simón